TEMPLE TALKS...

about Autism and the Older Child

The World's Leading
Expert on Autism
Shares Her
Advice and
Experiences

DR. TEMPLE GRANDIN

Author of *Thinking in Pictures*

Temple Talks ... about Autism and the Older Child

All marketing and publishing rights guaranteed to and reserved by:

A proud imprint of Sensory Focus, LLC

Phone and Fax: 888•507•2193

Online: www.sensoryworld.com

Email: info@sensoryworld.com

ISBN: 978-1935567646

Contents

Introduction

utism, a developmental neurological disorder, has a very wide spectrum. When kids with autism get older, they tend to fall into three different groups: completely verbal, partially verbal, and non-verbal with no useful speech. In my case, I had no speech until age four and then I became completely verbal. The first group of children (completely verbal) are either socially awkward with no speech delay or socially awkward with speech delay and then achieve normal speech. The second group (less verbal) may become partially verbal and the third group (non-verbal) never learns to speak. Within the non-verbal group, some children learn to type independently and have normal intelligence, and others have very severe impairments.

All children on the autism spectrum can benefit from good teaching. In elementary school, I had dedicated and experienced teachers who provided a structured environment. My ability in art was always encouraged. Educators should work to develop a child's areas of strength. Art class made school fun and art became the basis of my career designing livestock facilities.

My goal in this book is to lay out how best to transition an older child with autism into the adult world. Transitions are most effective when training for the next phase in life starts before a child graduates from high school. In my own case, learning to work started in my teen years. I had a seamstress job and I cleaned horse stalls. This taught me the discipline and responsibility of a job outside the home.

Temple Talks

about Autism and the Older Child

Building Social Skills and Doing New Things

Too many of today's kids are becoming recluses in their rooms. A psychologist recently described this phenomenon very effectively: There is a tendency for the world of a kid on the autism spectrum to contract. However, we must work to expand their world.

At the age of 15, I had the chance to visit my aunt's ranch. It was across the country and I was afraid to go. Mother gave me a choice: I could go for one week or stay for the whole summer. Not going was simply not an option. I went and it changed my life for the better. A whole world of opportunity and my future career opened up during that trip. So, as people, we have to expand our horizons; we have to stretch; we have to learn to be comfortable, and this has to start when we are still in school. I know a kid who was afraid to go to sleep-away camp, but his mom told him to go. When he got there, he absolutely loved it. I think we all have experiences like that. Once you stretch, you are glad you did. In both cases, the trip away was not a surprise. Surprises cause fear and panic. I was shown pictures of the ranch and had talked to my aunt, months before the trip.

The Importance of Shared Interests

I also emphasize the importance of social interactions based on shared interests: school, clubs, and activities. Parents often ask me about public versus private schools. I don't have a pat answer because so much depends on the particular school and the particular child. For example, one kid can do really well at a particular school, while another will be miserable.

Activities like Future Farmers of America are wonderful; so are Boy Scouts, Girl Scouts, and maker community groups. Maker groups are really cool; people get together and make all kinds of stuff—3D printings, robots. What if you live in a rural area? Well, how about fixing old broken lawnmowers? There's plenty of them and they're generally free. This brings up something else for getting kids motivated.

You have to show kids interesting stuff to get them interested and today kids are not being shown enough interesting things. Recently, I gave a lecture in a college class and the students asked me how I became interested in my passions. The answer is simple: I was exposed to cattle when I was in high school. People don't develop an interest in new things unless they are exposed to them. This is one reason why you have to get children out and try a lot of different activities.

Manners

Too many kids today don't know basic skills such as how to shake hands or say *please* and *thank you*. The parents do the talking for them, and they are not doing their children any favors. This problem is especially evident on the mild end of the autism spectrum. For example,

I went to a conference for the gifted and saw the same kind of geeky little kids that I see at autism conferences, but they were going down a really good path. Between the autism world and the gifted world, there is almost no communication but there are many commonalities; in fact, at the gifted conference social seminar, I thought, "Wait a minute; this sounds like an autism meeting." The autism and gifted programs really should be communicating with each other.

When teaching these kids manners, instead of screaming *no*, give instructions. If I ate mashed potatoes with my hands, my mother wouldn't scream *no*. She would say, "Use the fork." She would simply give the instruction instead of screaming no. That's the way to do it. All concepts are formed by specific examples. The concept of good table manners is learned by many specific examples where dining behavior is corrected. Over time, we learn how to act, and how not to act. Learning behavior over time is a very important concept.

The Importance of Structure in Teaching Living Skills

My 1950s upbringing really helped me with living skills. I went to college with a lot of people who would be labeled with autism or Asperger's today and they all got and kept jobs. One reason they're all employed is that in the 1950s and 1960s social skills were pounded into every single kid. We learned to take turns in conversations and activities and always to be on time. A college counselor told me that up to 70% of

college students on the spectrum have time management problems these days. For me, time management was easy because I learned to be on time for dinner.

However, some activities I didn't really like. I thought church was boring, but it's something the rest of the family wanted to do so I had to sit through it and not disrupt it. On top of that, I had to wear clothes that I hated. Sometimes, you have to do things that other people want to do. And this gets back to the fundamental principle of turn-taking. We played lots of board games in our family. This taught me how to wait and take my turn. If I tried to move a piece before it was my turn, I was calmly told to wait for my turn.

Fortunately, the church did not create sensory issues for me because it only had an organ. If it had been a blast-them-out-rock-and-roll church, it would not have worked for me. Let's say you go to a blast-them-out-rock-and-roll church; maybe your child can go up into the sound booth and adjust the volume; maybe they'd get to like the service if they could control the sound (you would try this during rehearsals, obviously). Children can often learn to tolerate loud sounds if they have control when initiating the sound. Another alternative is to allow the child to go into the lobby during the really loud parts.

All people have to learn basic social skills. For example, I don't know how many kids I've shown how to shake hands, applying just the right amount of pressure. I learned how to greet people with my brother and sisters when we acted as party hosts at my mother's dinner parties. We had to greet the guests and take their coats. While greeting guests, I learned how to shake hands. We also had to serve the snacks. Now, this is an everyday activity that any family can do. Everybody has parties, orders food in restaurants, and shops. Have your child learn to politely address the people around him or her.

My parents had about six parties a year. That was six parties a year where I could really get in some practice with my social skills. Mother would host about 20 guests and I had to shake hands with every single one of them and say good evening to them. This was really good experience for me. Assigning a child the task of party host or hostess is an easy and effective way to both teach and practice social skills.

Other skills that have to be learned are shopping and the meaning of money. I received fifty cents a week for allowance and I knew exactly what I could buy with it. In the 1950s, fifty cents could buy ten candy bars, five comic books, or a kite and string. If I wanted a sixty-nine-cent toy airplane, I had to save and have two weeks of allowance. Mother never bought these small items. I had to purchase them with my own money. The rules for shopping were also taught. The only merchandise I was allowed to touch was what I was going to buy.

Eccentricity Is OK

It's okay to be eccentric. It's not okay to be rude; don't try to de-geek the geek. For example, I recently met a lady who was wearing a beautiful pink 'Hello Kitty' outfit. Yes, it was very eccentric, but she looked really nice. I also met a lady with pink hair that was styled really beautifully. That's fine.

Many successful people are non-conformists. It's okay to be eccentric, but you cannot be a slob. One thing that worries me is seeing, for example, the guys at the Jet Propulsion Lab who are my age. They are eccentric geeks. What would happen to the younger version of these people today? Would they have a fun job where they're the navigator for the Mars rover or would they be playing video games in a basement somewhere?

Video Games and Tablets

I had an interesting talk with an organic farmer who would invite neuro-typical 10- and 11-year-olds to her walnut orchard to camp in tents. No screens or electronics. She said the kids, especially the boys, moped around for a while because they didn't have any video games or phones.

However, after about two days of video game withdrawal, she said a switch flipped and they discovered that climbing trees was actually fun. We have to get back to more free play. Kids lead such structured lives today that some of them do not know how to go about inventing or making their own activities.

I get many questions about the use of iPads and other tablet computers. A lot of great apps for tablets can replace bulky cardboard flashcards and communication boards for use with children on the spectrum.

Many children who have echolalic speech have learned to speak with the aid of flashcards; these children say words clearly but they may not know what the words mean. (These kids repeat lines from TV commercials and their favorite videos.) However, they can learn the meaning of words from flashcards. On a tablet computer, the picture of an object and the printed word for the object must appear on the same screen. The child must see the picture and the printed word at the same time to connect the object to the label.

A tablet computer is not a substitute for a teacher, however. To be effective, its use must be facilitated by a teacher or parent.

It is essential that the iPad not turn into just another way of doing stims (self stimulating behavior). I was allowed an hour every day for stimming; it helped calm me down. For the rest of the day, I had to keep my brain turned on. Keeping the child's brain tuned in for many hours each day is essential for development.

Companies come up with new apps every day. It would be impossible for me to keep up with every app available for tablets. You can ask other parents for recommendations and browse the Web. I typed "autism apps" into Google and found an excellent selection. Many of these apps replace cumbersome cardboard books and Velcro pictures.

Apps can be a great teaching aid for children on the spectrum, but I do not like some of the apps I have found. One was a replacement for a child's wooden puzzle. A motor component should be involved when learning shapes. The kids need to both feel and see the shapes. Only a physical puzzle or a set of blocks allows for that. Kids should learn about physical objects by touching and holding them.

In my own work, I have found perceptual mistakes on architectural drawings made by a person who had never drawn by hand or built anything. I saw these mistakes when the meat industry moved from paper drawings to computers. One draftsman did not know where the center of a circle was. To really understand this requires the motor component of drawing the circle with a compass. To prevent this problem, creative companies require some hand sketching. For example, Pixar has a three-dimensional printer that creates a plastic figure of the cartoon characters. Touching the plastic figures provides the important touch component of perception. Unfortunately, this type of printer is too expensive for most schools. However, modeling clay and blocks are within the budget and will serve the same purpose.

Credit: Walter Schneider
(University of Pittsburgh)

Figure 1: High-Definition Fiber Tracks of Temple Grandin

The Brain

Figure 1 shows the nerve fibers in my head. What you see highlighted is the connectome. This scan was taken by Walter Schneider at the University of Pittsburgh on the new state-of-the-art high-definition diffusion tensor imaging (DTI) equipment. The scan can track individual neurofibers in cable bundles of white matter. The fiber bundles form circuits that go between the different parts of the brain. This research was originally funded by the Department of Defense to study head injuries in veterans. In the future, this could be a great diagnostic tool for developmental problems; for example, the scan can determine exactly where a speech problem originates. Unfortunately, it is not available as a commercial diagnostic tool.

Figure 2

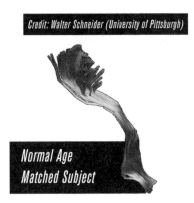

Credit: Walter Schneider (University of Pittsburgh)

Temple Grandin

Normal Age Matched Subject

Figure 1 shows my connectome without the rest of my head; on the edge are tiny single fibers. Those fibers are single axons that go all the way across the brain and form cable bundles. Figure 2 shows the normal circuit for "speak what you see." The circuit goes from the visual cortex of the brain up into the language area. From the image, you can see that I have a whole lot of extra branches. These extra branches go all over the entire brain, so when a keyword comes in I get a series of pictures. It's sort of like having a keyword system that works like Google for images. When I hear a word, my brain delivers pictures.

Now, at what point is an extra branch abnormal? There is no black-and-white dividing line for some of these things because they're developmental. The price I pay for having extra bushes is that I have less bandwidth to "speak what I see." In other words, I have fewer fibers to articulate what I see. I'm going to hypothesize that a child with echolalia will have this circuit as normal but will have problems in other kinds of circuits.

You can see the cable bundle for speak-what-you-hear in Figure 3. One can see I've got a little tiny shrimp right there; I am definitely not an auditory learner, though some kids with autism are.

Now, other research has shown that some social circuits in the frontal cortex, are not hooked up. Therefore, we should start looking at personality traits like a music mixing board. Each sliding switch on the board can adjust the volume of different personality or intellectual traits. We can amp up anxiety or lower its volume on each. You can make anxiety worse or make it better. Perhaps one brain tends toward problem solving and another is more social. When does normal variation become an abnormality? When do geeks and nerds become kids

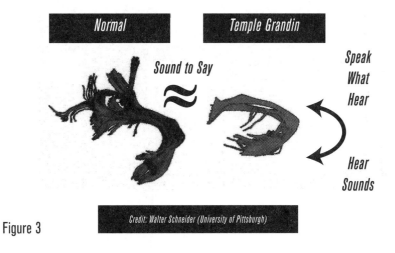

Figure 3

with mild autism? There is no black-and-white dividing line. I have traveled to Silicon Valley to a number of different companies, and, boy, I can tell you—no dividing line. There's mild autism all over the place. In fact, when you put a few of those computer scientists together, they can sometimes have kids at the more severe end of the spectrum. This is the big problem now. Autism is such a big spectrum, from a brilliant socially awkward genius to a person who is non-verbal and cannot care for him- or herself.

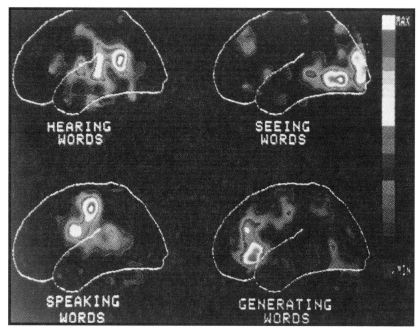

Figure 4

When you hear a word, see a word, speak a word, or think a word, different parts of the brain are engaged. You can see this in Figure 4. Circuits in the brain are required to connect these different brain departments. This is where you find abnormalities—in the interoffice communication between different parts of the brain.

My mind works like Google does for images. Figure 5 shows a picture from the *Little Rainman* book of a

Credit: Karen Simmons, Little Rainman

Figure 5

movie projector inside the boy's head. That is how I think—in pictures. I've had teachers ask me how to get pictures out of a kid's head. The answer is you can't. That is how some kids think. Being a visual thinker has really helped me in my work with livestock because I can test-run the equipment I have designed in my mind. I once thought everybody could test-run equipment in their mind. I didn't know my thinking was different until I started asking other people about how they thought.

Bottom-Up Thinking

How do I form a concept from all the different images floating around in my head? One young man sent me a picture to show how he makes different category boxes in his mind (Figure 6). In other words, he sorts pictures into categories. This is also called bottom-up thinking. In bottom-up thinking, concepts are formed by taking specific examples and sorting them into boxes. For example, I can sort cats and dogs into different boxes, or categories. I can also sort rude versus polite behavior into different boxes. All of this

Credit: *Karen Simmons*, Little Rainman

Figure 6

has to be taught by many different real-life examples. Let's say I spat on the sidewalk; Mother would say that's rude. Thus, I would learn that spitting is rude through a specific example. In another teachable moment, mother corrected me if I stuck out my tongue at a clerk in the store. Gradually, over time, I would gather many specific experiences that I placed in the "rude" file in my brain.

Thinking in Pictures

I really came to understand that my thinking was different when I asked a speech therapist at a conference to think about a church steeple. I was shocked to learn that she, like an awful lot of people, conjure a vague image of a pointy thing. I only see specific steeples; there is no vague pointy thing. My concept of steeple is based on lots of specific examples that I put in a file folder in my mind labeled steeple.

I also have another file folder in my mind of cellphone towers. I see the cellphone tower on the roof of the Hilton Hotel in Fort Collins; I also see the fake trees that are used to disguise such towers. This is specific. My images are triggered by search words similar to Google, but using pictures. Now I will open my church steeple file. First I see childhood images, then I see specific images in Fort Collins, where I live. I can sort them into different subcategories: famous steeples, local steeples, cathedral steeples, and chapel-type steeples. I have one big file folder for all steeples and then subcategories for different types of steeples.

To create those subcategories, I had to be exposed to a lot of different steeples. This ties into the importance of trying a variety of activities and doing a lot of things. It is important to get kids with autism out to experience the world to fill up their memory banks. I used to joke around and say that I have a huge visual thinking circuit that goes deep

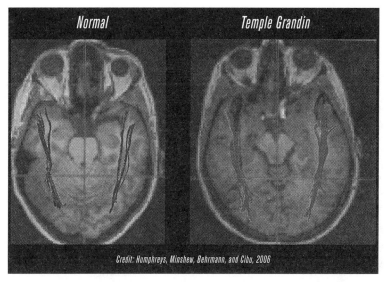

Credit: Humphreys, Minshew, Behrmann, and Cibu, 2006

Figure 7

into my visual cortex. Well, it turns out I do. It's not the biggest circuit; an art professor somewhere has a bigger one. However, I'm probably in the top 20%. In Figure 7, you can see it goes all the way back into the visual cortex.

How do you think about really abstract stuff when you think completely in pictures? When I was a young child, one of my first language assignments was to learn the Lord's Prayer. What's the power and the glory? Figure 8 is my picture for the power and the glory; we have a rainbow with an electric tower at the base of the rainbow. That's the power and the glory and this picture was not Photoshopped. It is real.

Photo Courtesy of Dr. Temple Grandin

Figure 8

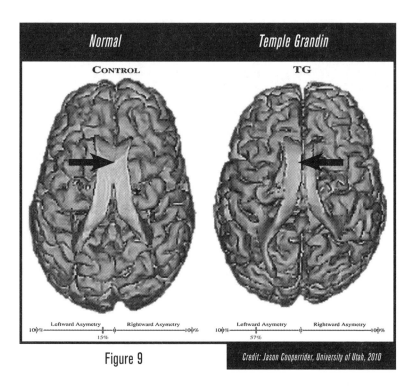

Figure 9

Credit: Jason Cooperrider, University of Utah, 2010

Figure 9 shows a scan which reveals why I was awful in algebra. The shaded part on this slide is full of water, cerebral spinal fluid, and you can see it pretty well trashed out the left parietal area. Thus, I have really bad working memory. This may be why many people with autism cannot remember long strings of verbal information.

Types of Thinking

I have learned from interviews with many people and scientific literature that there are four types of specialized thinking:

1. Photo realistic visual: good at art, photography, industrial design, computer graphics.
2. Pattern thinker: good at math, computer programming, engineering.
3. Word thinker: good at writing. Often loves history. Appropriate jobs would be journalist, fiction writer, and other writing jobs.
4. Auditory learner: learns best by what hearing rather than reading.

The brain has both what-is-something circuits and where-is-something circuits. My brain uses its what-is-something circuit to think in pictures. The mathematician uses circuits to understand where he or she is located in space. That's the mathematician's mind.

Industry needs visual thinkers. For example, the Fukushima nuclear power plant burned up because the personnel working there made a visualization mistake that was so obvious to me that I just couldn't believe it. Even though the plant was close to the sea, they put the super important generators for the emergency cooling system in a non-waterproof basement; if they had done something as simple as buying watertight doors from a ship-building company, the accident would not have happened. Electrical equipment does not work under water, so it is obvious that flooding must be avoided at all costs. I am not a nuclear reactor designer, but my visual thinking would have stopped that mistake. Visual thinkers are needed in this kind of job, especially in something so important as safety systems.

How to Determine Thinking Types

The types of thinking tend to show up in elementary school and may not be evident in very young children. For example, my artistic

Figure 10

ability was not obvious in first grade; it became apparent in third or fourth grade.

Figure 10 shows a picture that a young man drew when he was a very young child, in perspective. It is basic, but being able to show perspective at such a young age shows great promise. We have to build on these strengths. However, when do strengths start to appear? In most kids, it's around third or fourth grade. That's when my drawing ability became evident. Drawing ability will become apparent at that time, and mathematical ability will also show up at that time. With math, however, kids need to move ahead to more difficult problems because if they do the same boring math over and over again, they are likely to develop behavior issues.

Kids with my type of mind, visual thinkers, will draw lots of pictures. Both pattern thinkers and visual thinkers like to play with Legos. Word thinkers usually don't care much for Legos or for drawing. Pattern thinkers are often good at math if they don't have to show how they completed their work. That totally ruins it for them. This comes up in mathematics today because teachers want the kids to show their work. However, some of these kids can't do that because they think differently. I would still take precautions against cheating, but people can use different ways to do math. They can do it the verbal way or the more visual spatial way; each method will lead to the correct answer.

Look at Figure 11 to see what can come from the mind of a mathematician. This praying mantis is made from a single sheet of folded paper—no cuts, no tape. What you see in the background is the folding pattern. I look at that and can see that it's definitely not my mind.

I want to go back and review bottom-up thinking. This is really important. All my thinking uses specific examples to create concepts. That's the opposite of how most people think.

Most people form a hypothesis first and tend to over-generalize as they stuff their data into the hypothe-

Credit: Robert Lang, 2006

Figure 11

sis. I create the hypothesis by piecing together the many bits of data. This is bottom-up thinking, not top-down, and everything is learned with specific examples. Concepts are made up of specific examples. You can use games to categorize objects so that kids can learn things like color, shape, bigger than, and smaller than.

Some objects will fall into more than one category. For example, an object might be red and rectangular. Also, the brain of child with autism picks out the details. People in this spectrum are often really good with details.

Many people ask me whether autistic learning is just memorization and scripting. Yes, in the beginning it is. When I was in high school, other kids called me the "tape recorder." I could understand why they called me a workhorse, but a tape recorder?

Well, the reason they did is I always used the same scripts. However, if the child goes out and does more and more things, the child fills up the Internet inside his head with more and more web pages. That's why it's good to get kids out doing things. As you get more and more information loaded into the brain, think of it as filling up the brain's Internet; the brain is equipped with a really good Google for finding things.

Education

Build on Strengths

I cannot emphasize enough the importance of building on the kid's strengths. There is way too much emphasis on deficits and not nearly enough on strengths. My ability in art was always encouraged and I was encouraged to create lots of different kinds of pictures. Otherwise, I would have been drawing endless horse heads over and over again. Kids get fixated on their favorite stuff, so if the child likes airplanes, do math with airplanes or read a book about airplanes. You can teach just about any subject better using fixations.

Talking about fixations, one concern about the milder end of the autism spectrum is that too many older kids are fixated on their autism. They approach me at meetings and all they want to do is talk about their autism. Well, I'd rather hear about their science project or art project. When I was 10 years old, all I wanted to talk about was my kites and toy airplanes and things that I really liked. That's what they need to be focusing on. Encourage them to educate themselves about their autism and then to move on to what they love.

Bullying

What really helped me when I was bullied and teased in high school was hands-on activity. Suddenly I had interactions with peers who had similar interests, and these activities helped me make friends. The only places I was not bullied and teased were where I pursued special interests like horse riding, model rockets, and electronics. Kids need these specialized interests and one of the worst things the schools have done is take out all the hands-on classes: art, music, cooking, sewing, woodworking, metal shop, welding, auto shop. Kids need exposure to these areas because a lot of jobs are available for auto mechanics, electricians, and a lot of skilled trades. Smart people are required to perform these skilled trades.

Now, how can people deal with aggression? I had to learn. In ninth grade, I was kicked out of high school for fighting; when kids teased me, I responded with aggression. I had to learn to switch to crying. That's what NASA space scientists did when the shuttle was shut down. They cried and they didn't get angry. Interestingly enough, I once talked to two retired NASA space scientists who had grandkids on the spectrum; they said that half the people at NASA were on the spectrum!

Problems in Education

Today's emphasis on algebra likely screens out a lot of visual thinkers. When I was in college in 1967, we were in the finite math fad. Now we're in the algebra fad. In 1967, we studied finite math, matrices, probability, and statistics; this was a required class across the country and, with tutoring, I was able to do it.

Now, this is important. Kids labeled autistic, Asperger's, dyslexic, ADHD, or any of these different labels tend to have uneven skills. They tend to be good at one thing and bad at something else. Now, my mind works as a photorealistic visual thinker who thinks in photorealistic pictures; I'm what's called an object visualizer. An object visualizer will have trouble with algebra. Another kind of visual thinker is the pattern thinker. This is the mathematical mind, the engineering mind. These people think in patterns and often have trouble reading.

In my book, *The Autistic Brain*, I present scientific research showing that these two kinds of visual thinking really do exist.

Preparation for Employment

Preparing for employment is critical for teenagers. This preparation should start in middle school but it's never too late to start preparing. I had a great science teacher who acted as my mentor. He got me interested in studying; he got me motivated to study. We have to show kids interesting workplaces. We have to show kids interesting stuff to get them interested. I got interested in cattle because I was exposed to them when I was 15. Otherwise, I would never have had the career in which I have been so successful.

One idea is to bring trade magazines to the school library and let the kids look at them to see the variety of interesting jobs that exist. Other great resources are business magazines and professional journals such as *Science* and *Nature*.

Let's talk about some good jobs for middle school kids. How about walking dogs for the next-door neighbors? How about fixing computers at local businesses? How about creating PowerPoint presentations for business people? How about working on a neighborhood website? How about working in a farmer's market? Kids can pursue these types of jobs or maybe even something different like setting up chairs at a church on weekends. The job just has to be outside the home so the child can learn how to perform tasks when directed by somebody outside the family. When I was a kid, I cleaned eight horse stalls every day. I was proud of being responsible and taking care of the horses.

People can also just set something up in the informal economy. In some states, at age 14 you can work in retail stores. In other states, the age is 16. Regardless, it's good to develop some work skills when children are even younger than that. It can be something as simple as doing a small job for the next-door neighbors. It is important to remember that jobs help the most if they keep a regular schedule. You should be expected to show up at a certain time somewhere outside the home, and follow through with your duties consistently. This teaches the structure needed to eventually start a career.

Activities for Learning Adult Skills

Something like a robotics club is really great because kids have to work in teams. Another great activity is 3D printing. MakerBot 3D printing is another really entertaining thing to do. I always liked to show off my drawings.

Now, one of the things that I thought was interesting on the MakerBot website is its warning: Patience required. The other thing I liked about MakerBot is that is connects the computer world back to the real world. It is a machine, a little arm that squirts out plastic goo. If users get mad at it, it's probably going to print a blob of plastic goo rather than the desired item.

A lot of kids love the game Minecraft. I talked to one mom and she had a great idea. She went to the lumberyard and got a whole bunch of two-by-fours cut up. She brought them home and had the kids sand them and paint them in the Minecraft colors. Then all the kids in neighborhood were playing Minecraft in the driveway. Her kid became the hit of the neighborhood. These are ideas for activities that are easy to organize and carry out.

All kinds of educational resources are available. Community colleges have fabulous courses, so you should check them out. We need to think a lot more about getting kids into job prep.

Free Online Resources

Some great, free online digital resources such as programming classes can be found at Khan Academy. The hot computer languages today are C++, Java Script, Ruby, and Python. You can also take free programming classes at udacity.com. Another resource is codecademy. com. Options for younger kids are code.org and Scratch programming. New resources are coming online all the time.

If algebra is impossible, it should be skipped and the kid be allowed to move on to geometry. Many people find geometry easy even though they find algebra difficult. Geometry is visual. I went on Google images and searched to find links to many different visual geometry lessons. Searching Google images with the word trigonometry also produced sites for visual ways of teaching it. Even calculus as a search term produced some visual lessons.

Coursera.com offers free college classes. Wolfram Mathematica is also really a fun site. Many options are out there and carry the right price; they're free.

When I was in high school, I became fixated on optical illusion rooms because I saw one in a movie. The HBO movie about me shows the actual Bell Labs film that I saw in high school. Again, kids have to be exposed to interesting stuff to get them interested in interesting things.

Asperger's and Autism in the Workplace

At the HBO movie filming site, people with Asperger's and mild autism were everywhere and they were not in catering or performing menial jobs either. I saw a lot of older people in the mild spectrum in really great jobs doing really neat things. When I work on construction projects and visit tech companies, I see many people on the milder end of the autism spectrum who are undiagnosed. They are welders, metal fabricators, computer programmers, and electricians, and they also hold many other technical jobs. I want this for all kids as they grow up. Kids need to prepare for jobs they will enjoy, so they need to be exposed to a variety of professions.

I once worked in a plant in Tolleson, Arizona. How did I get that job? I met the wife of the company's insurance agent. There's a scene in the HBO movie where I walk up to the editor of *Farmer Ranchman* and get his card. I actually did that. How did I have the courage to do that? Well, I think it goes back to being a little party hostess. I knew how to introduce myself.

To get jobs, we've got to short-circuit some of the interview stuff and get really good portfolios together. When I met the wife of the insurance agent, I was actually wearing my portfolio, a shirt that I had hand-embroidered. I wore it to a cattleman's reception that we both attended. When I first started doing my design work, I sold my services to clients by showing them drawings and photos of completed projects. People thought I was weird, but when they saw my drawings, I got respect. Today, portfolios can be put on phones. I learned to have my portfolio with me all the time because I never knew when I would meet someone who was interested in having me do freelance work (Figure 12).

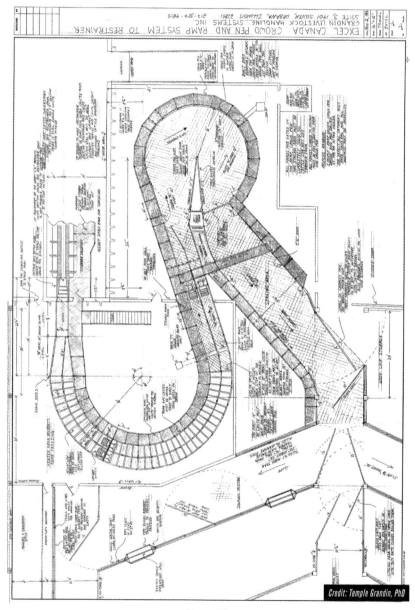

Credit: Temple Grandin, PhD

Figure 12

Right Jobs for the Right Kind of Thinking

What kind of job is right for my visual kind of mind? The answer is industrial design. Steve Jobs was an artist. An artist created the interface on every smartphone out there. Steve Jobs invented the interface and Samsung Galaxy copied it. That's the work of an industrial designer. Then the engineers had to make the inside of the phone work. Jobs designed the easy-to-use interface, and then the more mathematically inclined engineer actually got the thing to work.

For visual thinkers, good jobs would be in industrial design, computer hardware, graphic arts, repairing cars, fixing electrical wires, and setting up all the audio-visual equipment at big conventions. What about being a photographer, animal trainer, or a veterinary technician, which is a two-year degree at a community college? These are just a few of the jobs out there and there is a big shortage of auto and diesel mechanics right now.

Big pig farms need people who are good working around animals to work as stock people in the units that have group housing of sows. Farms are switching away from crates and the new systems require people who are intuitive with animals. Farm managers report that they need to find the right people to work with sows. A person who is calm and a bit different is ideal for teaching young sows to eat from electronic stations and finding sick animals.

How about jobs for our pattern thinkers and mathematicians? These people are our computer programmers, engineers, physicists, chemists, musicians, and math teachers. These are jobs for pattern thinkers. The tech world is really hot right now and there is a shortage of computer coders. Take some computer science, some electrical engineering, and some physics, and a little bit of mechanical engineering, and mix it all together, boy, you're going to be hot. Employers will hire you in a minute. How about the verbal thinkers? They might like professions in journalism or library science.

Verbal thinkers may not have a fancy portfolio of artwork or computer code to show off. However, one of the places they'd be really good is specialty retail. This is where we need to form alliances with retail stores. For example, workers who know everything there is to know about jewelry, men's shoes, or specialized merchandise, and this knowledge is valuable. However, these workers have to learn how to interact with customers. For example, they need to learn to approach a customer only twice and then back off. They will need coaching. Some verbal thinkers might be good writers and today all kinds of free self-publishing tools are available. However, it is important to only display your best stuff. Never publish rubbish online. I strongly recommend that any individual with autism get editing assistance.

How about people who have poor verbal skills? Walgreens redid all the computers in its warehouses so that people who couldn't read could work in the warehouse. The company hired people with different kinds of disabilities. You know what? The warehouses with the disabled workers are outperforming the others. We've got to start getting creative about job creation.

My mother likes to say it takes a village to raise a child. We have to figure out how to work together. Everything is becoming so bureaucratic, so just figure out things in the neighborhood; for example, set it up with the next-door neighbor to walk the dogs.

Careers

I have made a point of going to the tech community to give talks. I go to gifted conferences, autism conferences, and cattle activities and meat plant activities. A lot of old maintenance people in the meat plants are on the autism spectrum. During my long career, I have seen many undiagnosed older adults in various jobs. These jobs include computer programmers, welders, designers, and metal fabricators. I've observed that auto dealerships cannot get enough mechanics and factories have many jobs for people who are good at building and fixing equipment.

These workers have good jobs and enough social skills to survive different bosses. In fact, staying in one plant, or job, can be a good idea. I knew a man who was a brilliant electronics professional and his employer moved him to another plant. It was a disaster: He couldn't get along with his boss and his work and work performance really suffered.

People on the spectrum need the right kind of boss. An effective boss gives clear instructions that are never vague.

The big tech company, SAP, is now hiring people with autism to debug software because they're very, very good at details. If you show slides of different-sized letters, the person with autism will pick out the little letters faster than the big letters. There is also a company in Hollywood that employs people with autism to do computer animation for movie companies. They are using the attention to detail to the company's benefit.

During a long career, I have worked with many people who had classic signs of autism, but since they came from my generation they were never diagnosed. These individuals worked as equipment designers, welders, and millwrights.

Tips for Bosses

1. Written instructions work best. The endpoint of a good job and the deadline for getting a task finished should be clear.

2. Tasks that involve a series of steps should be written down with bullet points or a "pilot's checklist." Bosses should avoid giving long strings of verbal instructions.

3. A person on the spectrum may take longer to train, but will pay excellent attention to detail and remember all rules.

4. When social mistakes are made, bosses should be specific and tell the person exactly what he or she did wrong. Hints do not work. I had a boss who told me very directly to improve my hygiene and it saved my job.

Is Genius an Abnormality?

In today's educational system, Einstein would probably be labeled as autistic. He had no language until age three. Cavendish, the scientist who discovered the principle of electricity, was also likely autistic.

It is important for all the geniuses out there to learn to use their skills. It is important that every regular kid with autism learn to get out and eventually be employed and happy. I want all the kids who think differently to be successful.

Q&A

Questions and Answers with Temple

Q: Should my child be required to do chores around the house?

A: Yes. Doing chores teaches elementary school children important skills about doing work for others. When I was 13, I had my first job two afternoons a week. Below are all my work experiences before I graduated from college. Learning work skills is extremely important and work experiences should start in middle school. Today good work experiences for teenagers can be walking dogs, fixing computers, mowing lawns, making PowerPoint community presentations, and producing newsletters. Even volunteering at a church or similar organization can count as work.

My Teenage Work Experience:

- 13 years of age - Hand-sewed hems and took apart garments two afternoons a week for a freelance seamstress.

- 15-years of age - Took care of nine horses. I cleaned their stalls and fed them.

- 16 years of age - Worked on my aunt's ranch building a gate that could be opened from a car and other projects.

- In college, interned one summer in a research laboratory and rented a house with another lady.

- In college, interned a second summer at a program for children with autism and other disorders.

- In high school and college, freelanced as a sign painter.

Q: What is your best advice to parents of young adults at the low end of the spectrum who did not have early intervention by good mentors?

A: Many lower functioning individuals have severe sensory over-sensitivity. For example, they may not be able to tolerate a noisy restaurant or store. Some individuals are sound sensitive and others can see the flicker of florescent lights. Over-stimulation hurts and may cause outbursts or aggression. These individuals know the difference between a real job and fake busy work. An excellent behavior therapist told me that her client got angry when he had to set and unset a dining room table multiple times in a row. A better approach would be to teach him to set the table for each meal. Find tasks that the person can do that are useful tasks. Some individuals find heavy work calming. I have seen non-verbal individuals successfully cleaning horse stalls and doing household chores, yard work, janitor jobs, and other tasks.

Q: What is your advice to parents helping their teenagers transitioning to adulthood who are in the middle of the spectrum?

A: All individuals with autism, high, low, and middle on the spectrum, need to learn work skills. When teenagers are still in school, they need to learn how to do jobs such as walking dogs, picking up trash, or gardening. Individuals on the high end of the spectrum should start doing jobs that fit their skill area, such as art, photography, graphic design, computer programming, journalism, auto repair and maintenance, or retail sales. Transitions are most successful when the person transitions gradually from the world of school into the world of work.

Q: How can the school system better support high school students at the high end of the spectrum?

A: High school students on the high end of the spectrum need to learn work skills before they graduate. Some of the smartest people in the world have autism. Examples are Steve Jobs at Apple, Einstein, and Mozart. Children who are good at math can learn computer programming, physics, or statistics. The students need to learn how to do tasks other people want done. They should develop their innate abilities in art, math, writing, or music.

Q: How can parents and professionals best deal with aggressive behavior in adults with autism?

A: When I was aggressive, TV was taken away for one day. I also learned to control aggression by switching from anger to crying. Teasing, bullying, and being called names made me miserable when I was in high school. Aggression had consistent consequences. The rules were uniformly enforced by both my mother and my teachers. However, you should never take away activities that could become careers such as art, music, or computer programming classes.

Q: In many interviews, you mentioned the importance of "good mentors" and "building on their strengths." Can you clarify these two ideas?

A: *Mentor Teachers*

When I was in high school, I was constantly teased and my life was miserable. The only refuge from teasing was hands-on activity such as horseback riding and electronics lab. The children who liked these activities did not attack me with teasing. These activities were refuges from teasing. Mother was able to teach me to be on time and to have good manners, but she was not able to force me to study. I was not motivated to study until I had a reason to study. When I was in high school, I saw no point in studying. There were a few subjects where I got As, such as biology, and other subjects such as English and history in which I had no interest.

My science teacher, Mr. Carlock, was instrumental in motivating me to study. When I had returned from my aunt's ranch, I was fascinated with cattle squeeze chutes. A squeeze chute is a device for holding cattle still for their vaccinations. It consists of a metal stall with panels that squeeze the animal on both sides of the body. When I watched cattle going through the squeeze chute, I observed that they sometimes relaxed when pressure from the side panels was applied to their body.

Since I suffered from constant panic attacks, I tried getting in the squeeze chute. I discovered that pressure from the squeeze chute calmed my anxiety and nervousness. Unfortunately, many of my counselors and doctors thought that getting in a cattle chute was weird. After I built a squeeze machine that was similar to a cattle chute to calm myself, everybody wanted to take it away from me. I immediately became fixated on it and was motivated to prove that the relaxing effect was real.

Mr. Carlock saw this as an opportunity to motivate me to study. He told me that to find out why the pressure effect was relaxing, I had to study science. In my senior year in high school, I quickly improved my bad grades in English and history because I realized I had to pass these courses if I wanted to go to college and become a scientist. Mr. Carlock harnessed the tremendous drive of autistic fixation and used it to motivate academic study.

I will never forget the trip to the academic library with Mr. Carlock. During that trip, I learned that real scientists read journal articles written in scientific journals. I did not know what a scientific journal was. In the early 1960s, looking up scientific journals was hard. The psychology journals were indexed in large books of abstracts (article summaries). Since copiers were not available, each abstract that you wanted to keep had to be hand copied onto an index card and I kept all the cards in a recipe file box. In the late 1960s, when copiers became readily available, I was ecstatic when I could copy entire articles, which I carefully filed in loose-leaf ring binders. Scientific scholarship was hard, but my autistic tendency to fixate kept me going. My experience clearly shows how a creative teacher can really get a student turned around.

Learning useful skills that can turn into a career requires direction from a teacher. Today I have observed that individuals who have successful careers, such as computer programming, had a mentor or teacher to train them. Discipline is involved in learning a skill. In the technical fields, I have observed that very few kids learn high-level computer programming on their own. When left to their own devices, they tend to get addicted to video games and muck about on computers. They need assignments and guidance from a good teacher to learn career-relevant skills. In some families, the parents "apprentice" their kids into their profession. This has worked for many kids on the spectrum.

Q: What message would you give to families who are still suffering from lack of treatment and early intervention due to the absence of programs that help people with autism in our area?

A: This is a hard question to answer, but it is never too late to start teaching them. To foster pubic acceptance, we need to show the things that people with autism are really good at. One ability is amazing memory. Many individuals on the autism spectrum would be good in retail stores or in warehouses because they can remember information on all the products. In one town, an autistic man memorized where all the pipes were located under the streets. He would show construction crews the correct location to dig to avoid breaking the pipes. Another man works in an auto parts store and he memorized the product code for every item in the store. His knowledge was really useful when people were trying to find highly specialized parts.

Q: How are people with autism contributing to a better world?

A: People with autism contribute to a better world because people on the high end of the autism spectrum have invented large amounts of technology and art. I estimate that half the people in the computer industry have mild autism. They are less social, but they gain more ability to think. Autism is a continuous trait that ranges from Einstein to low functioning; genetics is a major factor in the cause of autism. Increasing scientific evidence suggests that mild autistic traits are related to certain types of creativity and intelligence.

Q: How were you able to overcome the bullies and the mean things that they said when you were younger and become so successful? I worry that the teasing will steal my daughter's self-confidence.

A: When I was in high school, I was bullied. The other kids called me workhorse and tape recorder. It was awful. I was able to overcome bullying by taking part in specialized activities; they were a refuge for me away from the bullies. Kids that did the bullying were never a part of these specialized activities. Some of these activities were riding horses, electronics lab, and the model rocket club.

Children with autism should be encouraged to get involved with peers who have the same interests as they do. Other great specialized activities are the drama club, music, band, computer programming, history clubs, karate, science projects, Lego robotics, and scouting.

Q: God has blessed you with a persistent mother. I have been pro-
foundly affected by the recent showing of the movie about your life
on HBO. My youngest daughter from as early as I could remember
has been a challenge. We have dealt with issues of sensory over-
stimulation. Learning was a challenge in that some matters had to
be explained multiple times and ways in order for her to understand. Anxiety was a byproduct of any and all issues above.

Have you ever felt, and at what point in your life did you feel, independent from your mother and do you recognize any specific mile-
stone in gaining that independence?

A: The feeling of independence was a gradual process over a period
of time. This process led me to independence that began after college graduation. People are always looking for a single big turning
point, but my development was a more gradual emergence.

Q: My autistic nine-year-old son is attending mainstream public school. He is very bright but is not performing well academically in class due to sensory issues. I have tried to address these issues with the school. What can I do outside school to help him understand his schoolwork? Should I get a tutor to help as I have been helping him myself?

A: Because your son is having difficulty academically, it would be a good idea to get him a tutor.

I had a tutor in college to help with math and French. I had extensive tutoring in math and statistics as an undergraduate and when I got my graduate degrees, I had three different math tutors in three different schools and they SAVED me. I found the tutors and started tutoring sessions before I failed the class. I asked for help after I got a bad grade on the first test.

To answer your questions about sensory issues, I do not have sufficient information. Sensory issues are very variable. You may want to read the companion volume of *Temple Talks* or my book *The Way I See It* for information on sensory issues.

Q: My brother (age 69) was diagnosed with Asperger's about 10 years ago. His very different ways were easy to detect when he was very young. Now he is starting to withdraw more and more into his very limited, routinized lifestyle. I think he would benefit from an Asperger's support group or perhaps a counselor very familiar with high functioning autistic adults. Any ideas would be appreciated. My wife and I have enjoyed learning about your life experiences. Your courage is inspirational. Thank you.

A: The best thing to do to help him would be to Google "Adult Asperger's Support Groups" in his area. This will give him the opportunity to meet up with people just like him. There should be many to choose from so he can find a good fit.

If you find there are not many groups in the immediate area, then check surrounding areas near the town where he lives. He should also get involved with a hobby where he can meet friends with a shared interest. My social life today is still centered around shared interests in animal behavior, the cattle industry, and academic research.

Q: I am working with a professor who is on the autism spectrum to assist her in organizing lessons and documents for clarity. Do you have any suggestions or resources to help?

A: You need to perform an editor's job on her class materials. Just the same as a book editor would for a book. Be specific, state what needs to be shortened, what needs clarification, etc.

You cannot teach in generalities. Point out why the work is too detailed, too long, mark up the handouts. Sit down with her one on one and help her re-write the material.

Be specific with instructions.

Q: My son has a problem with impulse control. He has a job at a fast food restaurant. He "knows" it's wrong to take a soda from work, but we caught him sneaking one out. He "dumpster dives" at his apartment even though he "knows" he could be stuck with drug instruments. He tells us in such a happy manner what he has found and he knows we will take it from him and trash it but he keeps doing it.

He just says he's sorry but nothing changes. Help.

A: Concerning the items that are taken from work, the food items that are taken without permission should be taken out of his paycheck.

I am not too concerned with the "dumpster diving." I have done it myself. One time I found a perfectly good chair for one of my students who didn't have any furniture in her apartment. When my sister and I were kids, we went trash canning and I found a really cool baseball game and a football shirt.

I would caution your son to wear heavy gloves and a jacket to avoid hurting himself. When I was a child, I only took good stuff out of trashcans. We knew which houses had quality trash and we did not go hunting in the yucky cans.

Q: How can I help my child become a successful adult like you?

A: Helping children on the autism spectrum become successful adults requires teaching them how to work. During their teenage years, having job experience, either paid or volunteer, teaches important skills. Before I graduated from high school, l had worked cleaning horse stalls, had a seamstress job, and worked on my aunt's ranch. All these experiences were outside my home, which helped teach me independence. My books, *The Autistic Brain* and *The Loving Push*, co-authored with Debra Moore, may be helpful.

Q: I am an artist and want to sell my work. Can you give me any advice?

A: You can put some of your best work up on the Internet. Make sure you only put up your really good stuff. You also need to get some experience working in a retail store, any retail store. This work experience will improve your social skills. I learned how to make really good portfolios of my work. When people saw my portfolio of photos and drawings, they were impressed. Today a portfolio can be put on a phone. You also need to create your own website. Other Internet venues for showing your work are craft sites, art forums, and LinkedIn, a business networking site. You must include an email address where people can easily reach you.

Q: How do you feel about violence?

A: I hate violent images in the movies. Since I think in pictures, it is difficult to get these images out of my memory. I do not want this bad stuff in my memory. Reading about violence does not upset me, it is seeing it. Cartoon violence and car crashes have no effect. The images I want to avoid are realistic depictions of torture and cruelty.

Q: You mention you have seasonal depression. How do you deal with it?

A: I use light therapy November, December, and January. I have a full spectrum LED lamp that I travel with and I use it for thirty minutes early in the morning. The principle is to artificially keep my days long. The light works best if I get up really early and use it before breakfast or showering. I have further details in my book, *The Way I See It*, 3rd edition.

Another thing I do every day is vigorous exercise. Doing 100 situps everyday helps me to be calmer and sleep better. Scientific research clearly shows that exercise is good for the brain.

Q: Who inspired you as a child?

A: When I was a kid, I admired famous inventors. My favorite book was about inventors. Some of the people profiled in the book were inventors of the steamship, sewing machines, rubber, grain harvesting equipment, and the telephone.

Q: What do you like to read or watch for entertainment?

A: I like Arthur C. Clark and David Brinn. I loved the movies *Avatar* and *Gravity*.

My favorite science fiction TV show was the original *Star Trek*. My favorite science fiction movies are *2001: A Space Odyssey* and *Avatar*.

For reading materials on the plane, I read *The New York Times, Wall Street Journal, The Economist, Business Week,* and many others. At home I read *Science, Nature, Beef Magazine, National Hog Farmer, Feedstuff, New Scientist,* and *The New Yorker*.

Q: How do you grasp the concept of God?

A: When I think about God, I see the vastness of outer space filled with galaxies. On my bedroom wall I have the NASA poster of the Hubble telescope Deep Space photo. It shows hundreds of galaxies.

Q: Are you okay with mistakes and criticism? Many young people with autism have trouble when they are not perfect.

A: The important thing is to learn from mistakes and not repeat them. When I was a child, I experimented with different kite designs to fly behind my bike. I had to try many different designs until I found one that worked. At an early age, I learned from the initial mistakes I made in the design. Children need to learn that sometimes they make mistakes and then work to correct them.

When I was young, I had problems with being criticized and I got really upset. Then I learned that there will always be some criticism. It is like Amazon book reviews. Even the best books will have a few negative reviews. I am happy if most people approve of what I do.

Q: You are famous for thinking in pictures. What is different about being a visual thinker?

A: Visual thinkers are usually good at art and drawing. Visual thinkers usually see pictures in their imagination when they access their memory for different things. Teachers and parents need to develop the skills the child is good at, because these skills can turn into careers. Visual thinking is described in this book.

Q: How do you know what kind of thinker you are?

A: My book, *The Autistic Brain,* has some tests in it to help you determine the type of thinker you are. Many people are mixtures. These thinking types usually show up between the ages of five and eight.

Picture Thinkers: Often good at art and poor at algebra. May be good at geometry.

Pattern Thinkers: Good at math and some children are good at music . These individuals may have difficulty reading.

Verbal Logic: Good with words and often loves history.

Q: What do you think about hippotherapy for older children?

A: Horses were my life in high school. Many kids with autism respond really well to horses. Parents have told me that their child said his or her first words on a horse. The combination of rhythm and balancing provided by riding calms the nervous system.

Q: Once I know what kind of thinker I am, does that determine what kind of job I should look for?

A: People on the spectrum often have uneven abilities. The visual thinkers, like me, are good at jobs such as graphic design and industrial design. The math thinkers are good at engineering and computer programming and the word thinkers are good at writing.

If a student is a visual learner they may be very successful if they choose a visual major such as art, industrial design, drafting, or architecture. Recording the lectures may help because then you can play them back. Many colleges have a disability office that can help student. My books, *The Way I See It* and *Different ... Not Less*, may be helpful.

The skills are uneven—good at one thing and bad at something else. I recommend that you look at my TED Talk from 2010 (www.TED.com).

Q: How do I meet people who also have autism or Asperger's syndrome?

A: I recommend that you join a local autism or Asperger's support group. You should be able to find a local one on Google. There are lots of good national Asperger websites such as Wrong Planet and Grasp Aspergers.

Q: I want to learn more, but am not quite ready to apply for college. Any suggestions?

A: I suggest just going and sitting in on a class. Steve Jobs did this in a calligraphy class and that is why computers have beautiful type fonts. There are lots of FREE online classes, especially in the sciences. Check out Coursera, Udacity, free classes at Stanford, MOOCs (massive open online classes), and Khan Academy.

Q: I am a teacher with several kids with autism in my Spanish class who are struggling. Can you give any guidance as to how to help them?

A: Some students on the autism spectrum excel in foreign language and others, like me, are terrible. French was my worst subject. Teach Spanish to the students who will be good at it. I was better off taking biology. My book, *The Way I See It*, will give you insights into the different thinking styles on the autism spectrum. If I had to learn a foreign language, I would need to first learn how to read in the language. My auditory processing difficulties would make it hard to learn by hearing. When I listen to Spanish, I hear gibberish and then I will suddenly hear a word I recognize. Words I have both read and heard are most likely to be recognized.

Q: You live alone as an adult, as does my son. Do you ever get lonely?

A: Eating by myself was lonely. You need to have lots of activities with people who have shared interests to make up for it. To be less lonely, I ate one meal a day in a restaurant.

Q: My son is an artist and I want him to get a job. Is there a job you would recommend where he can still use his artistic abilities?

A: Your son may be very good at technical drawing. You should definitely train the talent. He should also do drawing the old-fashioned way. Doing BOTH hand and computer drawing is best. There is a free program on the Internet called Sketchup for three-dimensional drawing. He will have a valuable skill if he can learn three-dimensional drawing on a computer. When he gets really good at this, he can then learn CAD drafting on an Auto Desk program. After he gets really good at drawing, he should start doing some freelance work. Many good forums exist online for showing portfolios. He can also take a class in entrepreneurship.

Q: My daughter has Asperger's and is very intelligent, but she has trouble communicating properly. Can you give us any suggestions?

A: With a highly intellectual student with autism who has poor verbal skills, it is good to encourage learning math and computer programming. There are free computer programming classes on Khan Academy and Code Academy. To become better at communicating, she has to get out and do it. Teaching her to communicate better is like teaching somebody how to behave in a foreign country. Maybe she should volunteer or get a job that requires communication, such as being an usher at a movie theater or church. She needs to be coached on how to behave at a job which requires communication with other people. Avoid the interview process. Work with a friend who can get her a job.

Author Bio

A Little More about Me

Favorite teams

I do not follow sports. Neuroscience, cattle behavior, and doing design work are much more interesting to me. As a child, I played tennis and loved to go skiing. As an adult, I lost interest in sports because I'm a bit clumsy.

Favorite books

I love science fiction for recreational reading. One of my favorite authors is Arthur C. Clark. When I was in elementary school, my favorite book was a little children's book about famous inventors. Unfortunately, I cannot find it on the Internet. Some of my favorite first-person accounts on autism and Asperger's are:

- *Be Different* by John Elder Robison
  Explains how he learned electronics and started his career.

- *Born on a Blue Day* by David Tammet
  Describes the mind of the mathematical pattern thinker.

- *How Can I Talk if My Lips Don't Move* by Tito Muchopadhyay
  An inside view of severe sensory problems in a non-verbal person who types independently.

- *Autism: An Inside Out Approach* by Donna Williams
  Provides insight into severe visual sensory problems.

- *Songs of the Gorilla Nation* by Dawn Prince Hughes
  Describes the author's gift for working with animals.

- *Thinking in Pictures*, my own autobiography
  Describes my successful use of antidepressants to control my anxiety.

Favorite business book

Tipping Point by Malcolm Gladwell. This book illustrates how change takes place. The work I did in 1999 for the McDonald's animal welfare program greatly improved animal treatment in meat plants.

Favorite book when I was in college

The Invisible Pyramid by Loren Eiseley. I kept this book through three different house moves.

Favorite books about animals

Black Beauty by Anna Sewell, *Merle's Door* by Ted Kerasote, *The Shadow of Man* by Jane Goodall, and *The Art of Racing in the Rain* by Garth Stein

Favorite music

"Stairway to Heaven" by Led Zeppelin. I also really like country western, classical, and oldies rock and roll.

Favorite movies

Avatar, *The King's Speech*, *October Sky*, *Star Trek* movies, *2001: A Space Odyssey*, *The Martian*.

Favorite TV shows

60 Minutes, *Big Bang Theory*, Classic *Star Trek*, *Star Trek: The Next Generation*, *Man from U.N.C.L.E.*, and *MythBusters*.

Who inspired me to succeed when I was young

William Carlock, my high school science teacher; Ron Kilgour, a livestock behavior researcher in New Zealand; and Ann Brecheen, my aunt out on the ranch in Arizona.

Favorite quotation

The following quotation has been posted on my wall since graduate school:

On Creativity
The person who follows the crowd will usually get no further than the crowd. The one who walks alone is likely to find himself in places no one has ever been before.

Creativity in living is not without its attendant difficulties, for peculiarity breeds contempt. And the unfortunate thing about being ahead of your time is that when people finally realize you were right, they'll say it was obvious all along.

You have two choices in your life; you can dissolve into the mainstream, or you can be distinct. To be distinct, you must be different, to be different, you must strive to be what no one else but you can be.

—Alan Ashley-Pitt

Education

High school: Hampshire Country School.
College: Franklin Pierce University, B.A. Psychology.
   Arizona State University - M.S. Animal Science.
   University of Illinois - Ph.D., Animal Science.

Employment

Professor of Animal Science, Dept. of Animal Sciences, Colorado State University. Also, independent designer of livestock-handling facilities. I have designed cattle-handling equipment for major meat companies. Served as a consultant on animal welfare for McDonald's, Wendy's, Whole Foods, and other restaurant and retailers.

Other Language

None. Foreign language was my worst subject.

Awards

Dr. Grandin has received numerous awards for her work on animal welfare; she has been recognized by both the livestock industry and animal advocacy organizations. She received many prestigious awards before she garnered recognition for her autism advocacy work. Colleges and universities have awarded her nine honorary doctorates and she is a Fellow of the American Society of Animal Science.

1984, Meritorious Service, Livestock Conservation Institute (now National Institute of Animal Agriculture)

1994, Golden Key National Honor Society, Honorary Member

1995, Industry Advancement Award, American Meat Institute

1995, Animal Management Award, American Society of Animal Science

1995, Harry C. Roswell Award, Scientists Center for Animal Welfare

1995, The Brownlee Award for International Leadership in Scientific Publication Promoting Respect for Animals, Their Nature and Welfare, Animal Welfare Foundation of Canada, Vancouver, BC

1998, Forbes Award, National Meat Association

1998, Geraldine R. Dodge Foundation – Humane Ethics in Action, Purdue University, West Lafayette, IN

1999, Humane Award, American Veterinary Medical Association

1999, Named one of the 26 Industry Influentials by *Meat Marketing and Technology* Magazine

1999, Animal Welfare Award, Animal Transportation Association

1999, Founders Award, American Society for the Prevention of Cruelty to Animals

2002, Richard L. Knowlton Innovation Award from *Meat Marketing and Technology* Magazine

2002, British Society of Animal Science, Yorkshire England, Animal Welfare Award Royal Society for the Prevention of Cruelty in Animals

2003, Western Section American Society of Animal Science

2004, President's Award, National Institute of Animal Agriculture

2004, The Beef Top 40: The 40 most influential people in the beef industry. Awarded on the 40th anniversary of *Beef* Magazine

2004, *Organic Style* Magazine's Environmental Power List

2006, *Animals in Translation*, a Top Science Book of the Year in *Discover* Magazine, January 2006 (p. 74)

2007, Autism Society of America Founder's Award

2007, Dept. of Health and Human Services, Secretary's Highest Award, Washington D.C. for work on autism advocacy

Association of Meat Processors, Meat Industry Hall of Fame, Chicago, Illinois

2009, Headliner Award, Livestock Publications Council, Fort Worth, Texas

2010, Fellow – American Society of Animal Science

2010, Inducted into the National Cowgirl Hall of Fame in Dallas, Texas

2010, National Cattlemen's Beef Association – Lifetime Achievement Award

2010, *Time* Magazine – One Hundred Most Influential People, Heroes Category

2011, American Humane Association, Humanitarian Award

2011, Hall of Great Westerners, Oklahoma State University

2011, The Halal Journal Award

2011, Friend of Occupational Therapy, Department of Occupational Therapy, Colorado State University

2011, American Meat Science Association Special Recognition

2013, National 4H Distinguished Alumni Medallion

2015, OIE World Organization of Animal Health, Paris, France; Meritorious Award for work on international animal welfare guidelines

A complete list of awards is on www.grandin.com.